AF261518

Taylor's STEM
Adventures Texas

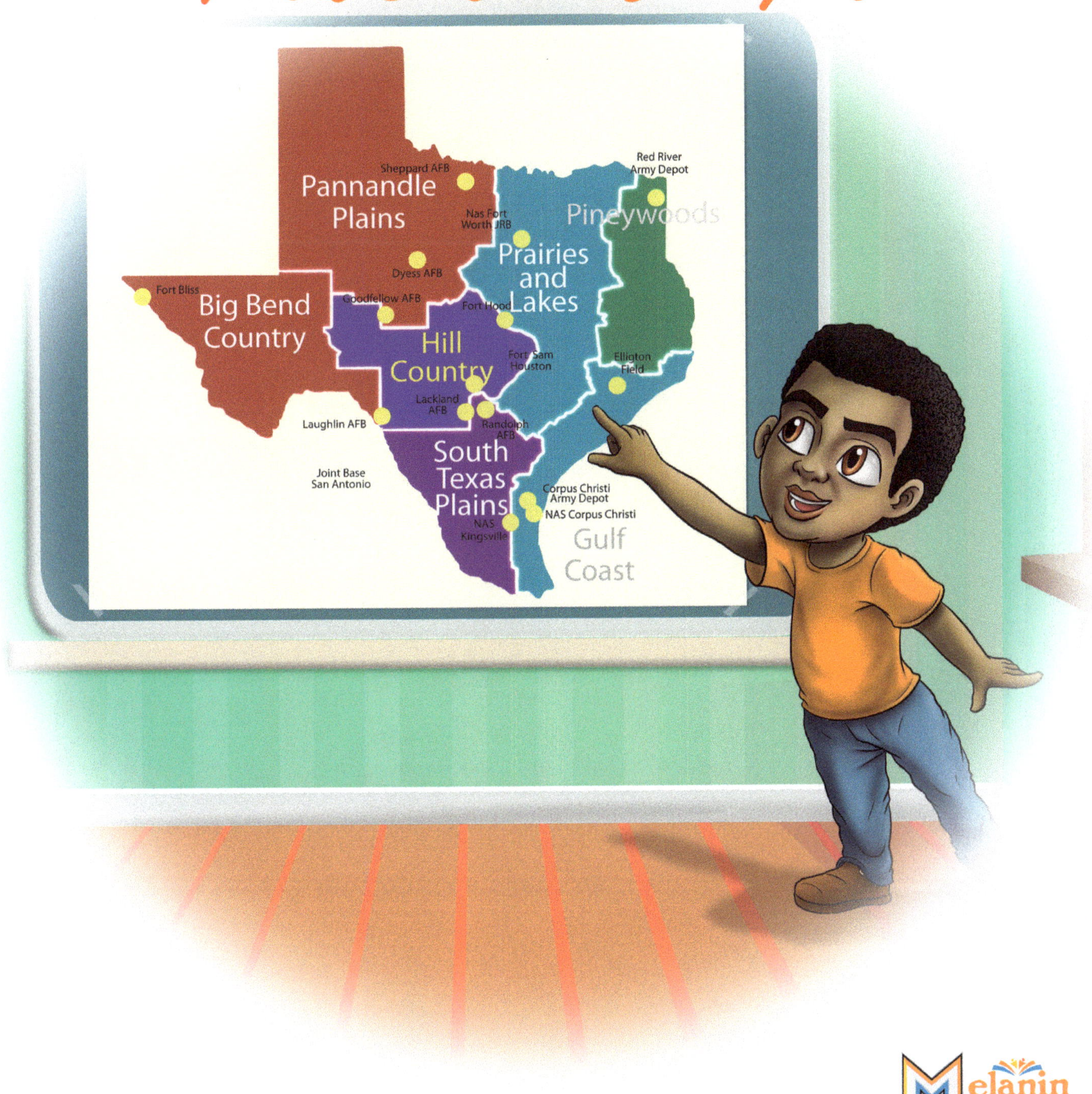

By: Dr. Mary Payton

Published by Melanin Origins LLC
PO Box 122123; Arlington, TX 76012
All rights reserved, including the right of reproduction in whole
or in part in any form.
Copyright 2019

First Edition

Library of Congress Control Number: 2018962597

ISBN: 978-1-62676-131-5 hardback
ISBN: 978-1-62676-130-8 paperback
ISBN: 978-1-62676-132-2 ebook

This book is dedicated to Mr. Hernán Contreras a great Mexican American mathematician, a proud military officer and NASA engineer. Thank you for being a part of Taylor's story. Also to my sons Taylor and Aaron who continue to make me a proud military mother. Thank you for your support and encouragement. Furthermore to my sister Peggie Wimbish for supporting my military career.

Finally I dedicate this book to all children who have parents that proudly serve as part of the Armed Forces. You are a big part of our careers in addition to making every move a great adventure.

Dr. Mary Payton

Howdy! My name is Taylor, and these are my STEM adventures. STEM stands for Science, Technology, Engineering and Mathematics.

My parents are both in the U.S. Army, working as STEM officers. My mom is a Chemical Officer and my dad is an Engineer Officer. Since science and engineering go hand in hand, my parents encourage and inspire me to grow my STEM talents. Because my parents are in the military, we have the chance to live and visit exciting places. Our new job is at Fort Sam Houston in San Antonio, Texas.

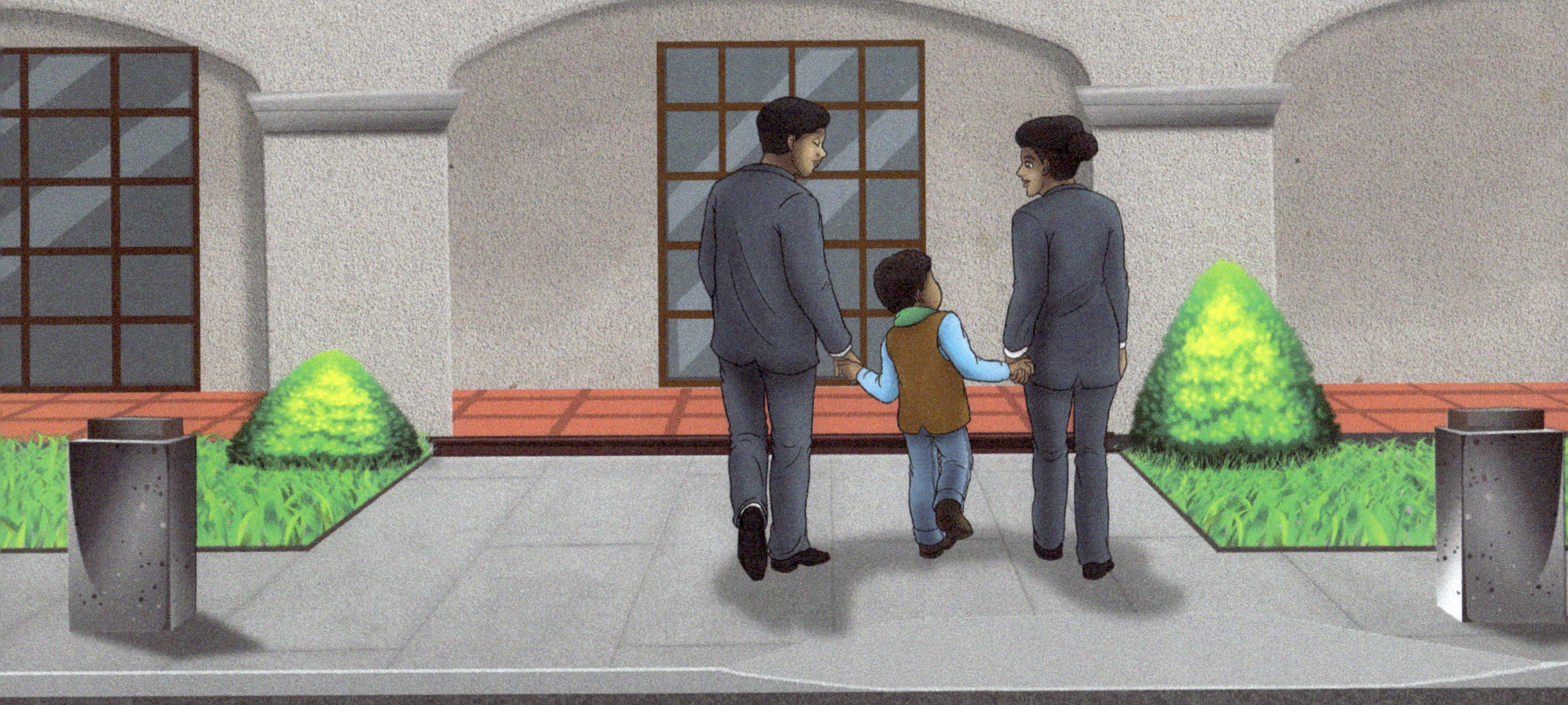

WELCOME TO FORT SAM HOUSTON
HOME OF THE COMBAT MEDIC

Texas is the second largest state in the United States of America. The state is smaller than Alaska but bigger than California. Texas is made up of seven regions. These regions include South Texas Plains, Gulf Coast, Piney Woods, Hill Country, Big Bend Country, Panhandle, and Prairies-Lakes.

Texas has been at the forefront of STEM for many years. It not only has many military bases, Texas also has many STEM things to do, and interesting places to see. Can I tell you about some that I like?

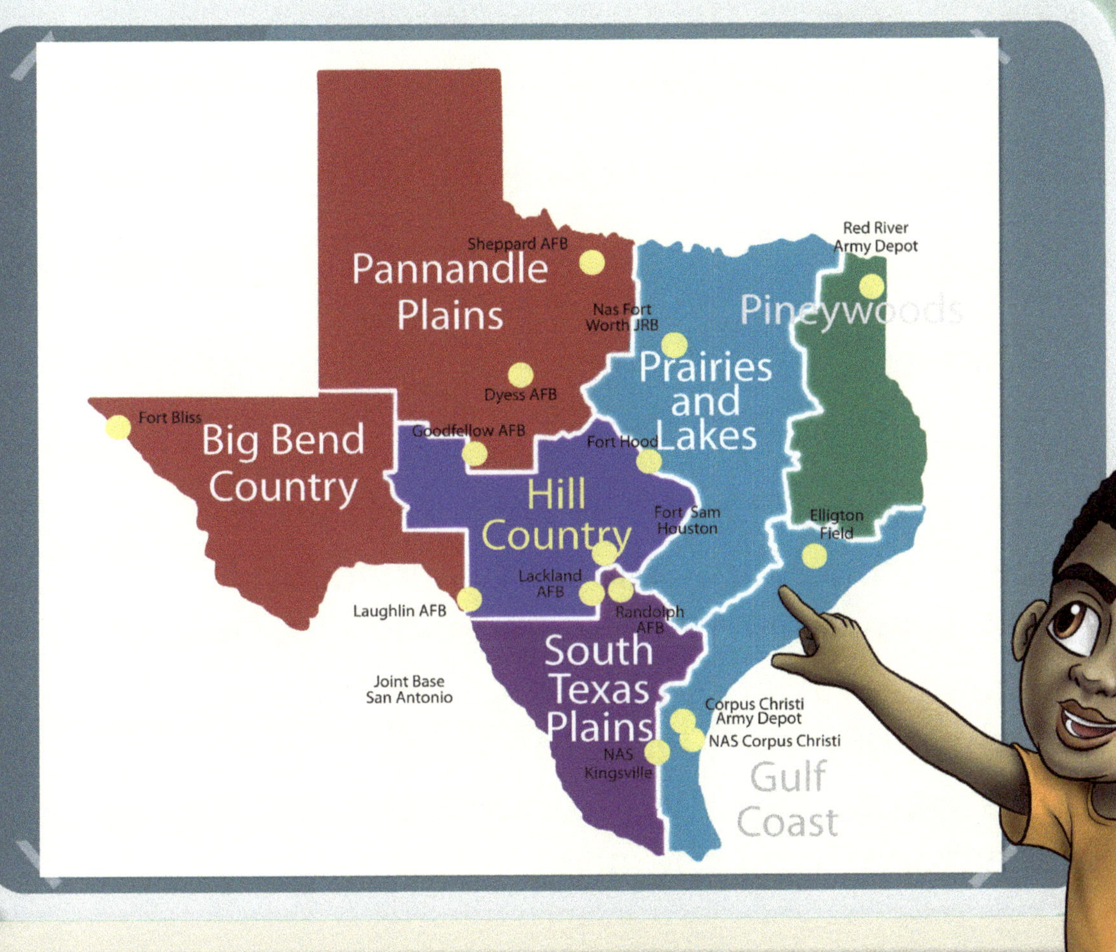

Sheppard AFB
Red River Army Depot
Pannandle Plains
Nas Fort Worth JRB
Pineywoods
Dyess AFB
Prairies and Lakes
Fort Bliss
Goodfellow AFB
Fort Hood
Big Bend Country
Hill Country
Fort Sam Houston
Elligton Field
Lackland AFB
Laughlin AFB
Randolph AFB
South Texas Plains
Joint Base San Antonio
Corpus Christi Army Depot
NAS Corpus Christi
NAS Kingsville
Gulf Coast

First, San Antonio has great historical architecture throughout the city. Places I visited with mom and dad include the San Antonio Missions National Historical Park, the Alamo, and the Fort Sam Houston Quadrangle. These places were built over a hundred years ago with limestone from the area.

Limestone is a type of sedimentary rock formed by the buildup of sediments during the rock cycle. This sediment comes from deposits of the remains of sea organisms, such as shellfish and corals.

Why do you think many of the historic buildings in Texas are made of limestone? The reason limestone was used in many Texas buildings is because it was a material that was handy.

Melting
Cooling & Melting
Rock Cycle
Metamorphic Rock
Igneous Rock
Heat & Pressure
Weathering & erosion
Sedimentary Rock
Sediment
Build up & hardening

One day my dad asked me, "What does Disneyland and the San Antonio River Walk have in common?" Dad explained that the original River Walk was engineered for flood control after the 1921 flood. It is a beautiful 15-mile long park with five miles of the River Walk passing through downtown San Antonio.

So, I asked dad, "What does the River Walk have in common with Disneyland?" He said it was the engineers. The engineering company that designed Disneyland suggested that the River Walk reflect a Mexican colonial design. That is why it is so beautiful.

In school, our teacher told us about a number of caverns around Texas. According to him, Texas is a beautiful state above and below ground. It has more than 60 caverns and caves that have unique geological features and creatures.

During dinner, I told mom and dad about the beautiful underground caverns near us. Mom asked if I knew how they were made, and I said, "Yes! Can I tell you?" She nodded, so I told her that the caverns were made by underground water moving through the limestone and flowing down from cracks in the surface.

I explained that this flowing water created interesting formations called stalactites and stalagmites. Also that these formations looked like icicles: stalactites growing down from the ceiling; and stalagmites growing upward from the cavern floor.

The creatures living in the caverns are cave beetles, spiders, crickets, cascade salamanders, and bats. Some creatures never leave the caverns and have adaptations that help them to live in the dark. Because of the dark, many cave creatures do not have to camouflage themselves, so they have light coloring.

One weekend mom, dad and I visited the Natural Bridge Caverns in San Antonio. We toured the underground caves to see the geological formations. Even though it was hot outside, it was cool and humid inside the cavern. The guide told us that the temperature was 70 degrees year-round, with 99 percent humidity. Because of the humidity, the stalactite and stalagmite formations were still growing. There were many rooms in the cavern. My favorite was the Hall of the Mountain Kings. It was as big as a football field!

One week my mom had to go to work in Austin, which is the capital of Texas. Austin is near San Antonio, so my Aunt Morgan and I went with her on the trip. As we got into Austin, I saw a huge pink building. I asked mom, "Why is the building pink?" She was not sure, so we called dad to ask about the building. Dad told us that this was the Texas Capitol Building. The Capitol was built with Sunset Red granite because there was a problem with the local limestone. The Sunset Red granite gave the building its pink color.

While mom worked, my aunt and I visited different places in Austin. Austin has a number of museums, parks, libraries, and more. One place that Aunt Morgan and I visited was Mount Bonnell, also called Covert Park. It is located beside the Lake Austin part of the Colorado River. We walked up the 102 steps to the top to see the river and the city of Austin. But we both had more fun at the Austin Nature and Science Center because we could touch everything. It was a great place, and admission was free!

In school, we learned that Austin had the largest number of Mexican free-tailed bats in any urban area. But Bracken Cave, 70 miles south of Austin, had the largest bat colony in the world. Chiropterologists are the scientists who study bats. There must be a lot of these scientists working in Austin because the city has one and a half million bats living there.

On our last evening in Austin, we went to the Congress Avenue Bridge area to do some shopping. Mom had a big surprise for us while we were there. Just before sundown, we went to sit near the bridge with lots of other people. As the sun started to set, hundreds and hundreds of bats began to fly out of the spaces under the bridge, and headed eastward. It was amazing!

I told dad all about the trip when we returned home. He enjoyed our talk and agreed that we must visit Austin again. During our talk, dad asked me what I knew about dinosaurs. I told him that dinosaurs were huge and ate meat and plants, and also were extinct. He answered, "Yes they are." Next, dad asked, "Were there dinosaurs in Texas?" I had to think before I answered him. Then I said yes, because on a school visit to the Witte Museum, we learned about fossils at the dinosaur gallery.

Dad told me that around 110 million years ago, over 25 different dinosaurs and prehistoric animals lived in Texas. Many of them lived in areas between San Antonio and Fort Worth, as well as in the Big Bend National Park. According to dad, the dinosaurs that eat meat are called carnivores, and those that eat plants are called herbivores. But he also said that there were omnivores, which are dinosaurs that eat both meat and plants.

Because Aunt Morgan lives in Fort Worth, I asked my parents if we could stop to see the dinosaurs when they took her home. They agreed, and mom helped me choose places to visit on our trip. Our first stop was Waco, Texas to visit the Waco Mammoth National Monument. In 2015, the monument became part of the Texas National Park System through an executive order signed by President Barack Obama.

Ft. Worth
Dallas
Glen Rose
Fort Worth
El Paso
Waco
Austin
Big Bend Nat'Park
San Antonio
Houston

The Waco Mammoth National Monument is the home of the Columbian Mammoth and other Ice Age animals. The Columbian Mammoth is not a dinosaur, but a prehistoric animal from the same family as the elephant. At the monument, we were able to tour the Dig Shelter to see fossils as they were found by paleontologists.

Our next stop was Glen Rose, which was out of the way, so we stayed the night there. In Glen Rose, we visited the Dinosaur Valley State Park. There in the riverbed we saw fossilized tracks from Theropods and Sauropods. The Theropods were two-legged carnivores with sharp claws, and the Sauropods were four-legged herbivores. A park ranger told us that the Sauropods footprints looked like big, bear tracks, and their handprints were round like elephant tracks.

It was a great trip!

During the ride to Fort Worth, Aunt Morgan told me about the Pawpawsaurus. The Pawpawsaurus was a species of dinosaur found in Tarrant County where she lives. The dinosaur skull was found in 1992 and looked like a big armadillo. There is no relationship between the Pawpawsaurus, a 15-foot long dinosaur, and the armadillo, which is a mammal. The Pawpawsaurus skull fossil is on display at the Fort Worth Museum of Science and History. I asked Aunt Morgan if we could go to the museum during our visit. She agreed that we should go.

Aunt Morgan is a math teacher, and works in a university pre-engineering program. Because it was summer, I was staying with her for two weeks. I asked Aunt Morgan, "Can I go to work with you?" Aunt Morgan said, "Yes. You'll go to work with me, and I'm sure you'll have a great time."

1) 5r -1+8s-2s-2r
3 -(2)+6 -1)-1
Ans=-13
2) 9+2(4+3)
9+2(7)
Ans=23
3) Fiind the exact value of cot(420)

Going to work with Aunt Morgan, I was able to learn how to build bridges and robots. We also went to places like Lockheed Martin and the Texas Motor Speedway. But our visit to the Fort Worth Museum of Science and History was my favorite. I not only saw dinosaurs and the energy exhibits, but also visited the planetarium, which was just wonderful!

Aunt Morgan told me that San Antonio was near Houston, and that maybe my parents would take me to visit NASA sometime.

Pre-eng
Pre-eng
Pre-en

Lucky for us, during a trip to the Gulf Coast we met Mr. Hernán Contreras in Houston. Mr. Contreras is the uncle of one of mom's friend who is a retired NASA engineer. He is a Mexican American mathematician who graduated from Texas A&M University. Mr. Contreras took us to see the Saturn V rocket at the NASA Johnson Space Center.

Mr. Contreras also told us that the Saturn V rocket was used during the Apollo missions to take American astronauts to the Moon. Because of the Saturn V rocket, the Apollo spacecraft and the lunar lander were able to make moon landings. Over a five-year period, the rocket launched 27 astronauts into space, with six moon landing missions.

Mr. Contreras is also an amateur astronomer, and a member of the Johnson Space Center Astronomical Society. That night, we stargazed using the Newtonian telescope that he himself built. Through the telescope, we could see stars and constellations close up.

We had a great trip to the Texas Gulf Coast. I will tell you more about it later. Texas is such a big state, and we will be here for a long time. I hope you enjoyed hearing about my adventures because I have more STEM Adventures to share with you.

Adiós until next time, Y'all!

All of the facts found in this book have been verified using the History of the River Walk, Natural Bridge Caverns, the websites for Prehistoric Texas, and the Saturn V Rocket at NASA Johnson Space Center, and the Houston Astronomical Society Guide Star, February 2014.

 Vocabulary

Adaptations - The act of adapting or adjusting.

Astronauts - A person who is trained to travel in a spacecraft.

Astronomer - A scientific observer of the celestial bodies.

Camouflage - The process of animals changing their colors, patterns, and shapes to disguise them from predators or prey.

Geological - Referring to the study of the Earth and what it is made of.

Fossil - The remains or traces of plants and animals that lived long ago.

Granite - A hard, igneous rock that is used in building projects.

Humidity - The amount of water vapor in the air.

Limestone - A type of rock that is made up of bits of animal shells.

Mammal - Animals with fur or hair that feed milk to their young and whose babies are born alive.

Paleontologist - The scientist who studies the forms of life existing in earlier geological periods, as represented by their fossils.

Rock cycle - Rocks changing from one form into another in a never-ending series of processes.

Rocket - A space capsule or vehicle put into orbit by such devices.

Sediment - Pieces of material carried and deposited by water or wind.

Sedimentary rocks - Rocks made up of bits of rock joined together.

Spelunking - Exploring caves, especially as a hobby.

Stalactites - Deposits of calcium carbonate resembling icicles hanging from the roof or sides of a cavern.

Stalagmites - Deposits of calcium carbonate like inverted stalactites formed on the floor of a cave by the drip of water.

Temperature - The measure of how cold or how hot someone or something is.

About the Author

Dr. Mary Payton is a science and STEM (Science, Technology, Engineering and Math) education professional who has taught throughout the United States and internationally. She returned to STEM education after a successful 29 year military career as an Army Chemical Officer. After retiring as a Lieutenant Colonel, Dr. Payton and her two sons moved to her home in Texas to teach science. Dr. Payton has been honored for her performance as a STEM educator in the areas of Robotics and Engineering. Due to military families relocating about every three years, Dr. Payton exposed her children to STEM at every duty station. Because of these experiences she was motivated by her family and friends to write "Taylor's STEM Adventures", a book series chronicling STEM activities focused on military family's relocations and travel.